W9-AYG-031

KOKOMO SCHOOL BOOKSTORE RENTAL BOOK

1. This book is not to be bought or sold.
2. Do not use this book to carry loose paper, notebooks, or pencils.
3. Do not mark in this book, or mutilate it in any way.
4. If this book is lost or damaged, the one renting it will be held responsible.
5. No book will be rented for a longer time than one school year.
6. Pupils moving from the city or withdrawing from school must return all rental books before leaving.
7. Pupils failing to return any rental book will be denied the right to rent books in the future.

TREASURY OF LITERATURE

WHISPER A SONG

SENIOR AUTHORS
ROGER C. FARR
DOROTHY S. STRICKLAND

AUTHORS
RICHARD F. ABRAHAMSON
ELLEN BOOTH CHURCH
BARBARA BOWEN COULTER
BERNICE E. CULLINAN
MARGARET A. GALLEGO
W. DORSEY HAMMOND
JUDITH L. IRVIN
KAREN KUTIPER
DONNA M. OGLE
TIMOTHY SHANAHAN
PATRICIA SMITH
JUNKO YOKOTA
HALLIE KAY YOPP

SENIOR CONSULTANTS
ASA G. HILLIARD III
JUDY M. WALLIS

CONSULTANTS
ALONZO A. CRIM
ROLANDO R. HINOJOSA-SMITH
LEE BENNETT HOPKINS
ROBERT J. STERNBERG

HARCOURT BRACE & COMPANY
Orlando Atlanta Austin Boston San Francisco Chicago Dallas New York
Toronto London

Copyright © 1995 by Harcourt Brace & Company

All rights reserved. No part of this publication may be reproduced or transmitted in any form or by any means, electronic or mechanical, including photocopy, recording, or any information storage and retrieval system, without permission in writing from the publisher.

Requests for permission to make copies of any part of the work should be mailed to: Permissions Department, Harcourt Brace & Company, 6277 Sea Harbor Drive, Orlando, Florida 32887-6777.

Portions of this work were published in previous editions.

Printed in the United States of America

ISBN 0-15-301247-1

4 5 6 7 8 9 10   032 97 96 95

Acknowledgments

For permission to reprint copyrighted material, grateful acknowledgment is made to the following sources:

Curtis Brown, Ltd.: "Counting" from *Side By Side: Poems To Read Together* by Lee Bennett Hopkins. Text copyright © 1987 by Lee Bennett Hopkins. Published by Simon & Schuster. "I Eat My Gumdrops" from *I Was Thinking* by Freya Littledale. Text copyright © 1979 by Freya Littledale. Published by Greenwillow Books.

Childrens Press: Cover illustration by Dennis Hockerman from *The Little Red Hen* by Patricia and Fredrick McKissack. Copyright © 1985 by Regensteiner Publishing Enterprises, Inc.

Child's Play (International) Ltd.: *Quick as a Cricket* by Audrey Wood, illustrated by Don Wood. © 1982 by M. Twinn.

Chronicle Books: *My Friends* by Taro Gomi. Copyright © 1989 by Taro Gomi; English text copyright © 1990 by Chronicle Books. Originally published in Japan by Ehonkan Publishers, Tokyo.

The Lois Lenski Covey Foundation, Inc.: From "All the People on Our Street" in *City Poems* by Lois Lenski. Text copyright © 1971 by Lois Lenski.

Delacorte Press, a division of Bantam Doubleday Dell Publishing Group, Inc.: Cover illustration from *Hold Tight, Bear!* by Ron Maris. Copyright © 1988 by Ron Maris. Originally published in Great Britain by Julia MacRae Books, a division of Walker Books, Ltd.

Dutton Children's Books, a division of Penguin Books USA Inc.: "Jump or Jiggle" by Evelyn Beyer from *Another Here and Now Story Book* by Lucy Sprague Mitchell. Text copyright 1937 by E. P. Dutton, renewed © 1965 by Lucy Sprague Mitchell.

Mari Evans: "I Can" from *Singing Black* by Mari Evans. Text copyright © 1976 by Mari Evans. Published by Reed Visuals, 1979.

Greenwillow Books, a division of William Morrow & Company, Inc.: Cover illustration from *Flying* by Donald Crews. Copyright © 1986 by Donald Crews.

Harcourt Brace & Company: Cover illustration by Jeni Bassett from *But Not Like Mine* by Margery Facklam. Illustration copyright © 1988 by Jeni Bassett. *I Went Walking* by Sue Williams, illustrated by Julie Vivas. Text copyright © 1989 by Sue Williams; illustrations copyright © 1989 by Julie Vivas. *Silly Sally* by Audrey Wood. Copyright © 1992 by Audrey Wood.

Macmillan Publishing Company, a division of Macmillan, Inc.: Cover illustration from *Rosie's Walk* by Pat Hutchins. Copyright © 1968 by Patricia Hutchins.

MGA, Inc.: Lyrics from "Willoughby, Wallaby, Woo," based on "Alligator Pie" by Dennis Lee. Lyrics copyright © by Dennis Lee.

Illustration Credits

Key: (t) top, (b) bottom, (c) center.

Table of Contents Art

Thomas Vroman Associates, Inc., 4, 5

Bookshelf Art

Thomas Vroman Associates, Inc., 6, 7

Theme Opening Art

Robert Frank, pages 8, 9; Ben Mahon, pages 78, 79

Selection Art

Don Wood, 10–40; Jennie Oppenheimer, 41; Taro Gomi, 42–72; Tuko Fujisaki, 73; Audrey Wood, 80–110; Sal Murdocca, 111; Keaf Holliday, 112–113; Julie Vivas, 115–144

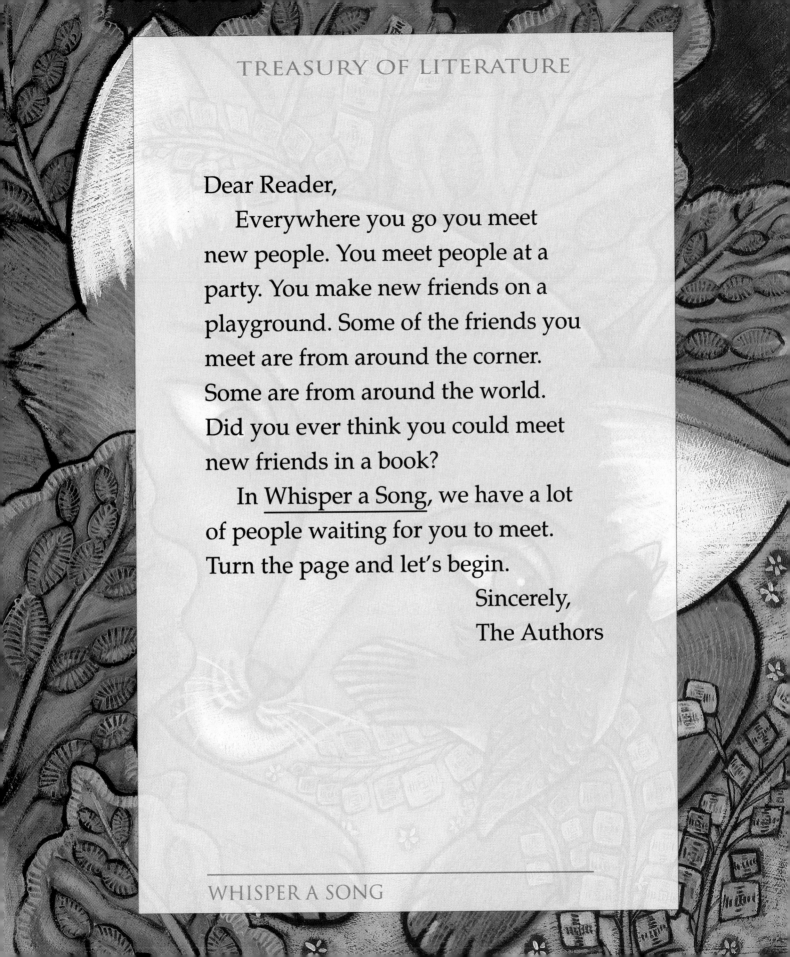

Dear Reader,

Everywhere you go you meet new people. You meet people at a party. You make new friends on a playground. Some of the friends you meet are from around the corner. Some are from around the world. Did you ever think you could meet new friends in a book?

In Whisper a Song, we have a lot of people waiting for you to meet. Turn the page and let's begin.

Sincerely,
The Authors

CONTENTS

BOOKSHELF

HOLD TIGHT, BEAR!

by Ron Maris

"Bear and Raggety, Little Doll and Donkey, are going for a picnic." You can go along with them. Find out what happens to Bear when his friends fall asleep. How will Bear's friends help him?

Harcourt Brace Library Book

FLYING

written and illustrated by Donald Crews

Climb aboard an airplane and get ready to fly. There are many exciting things to see from high up in the sky.

New York Times Best Illustrated
Harcourt Brace Library Book

ROSIE'S WALK

by Pat Hutchins

Rosie the hen goes for a walk. She doesn't know that a fox is following her. Will the fox catch Rosie? Find out by reading this book.

ALA Notable Book

THE LITTLE RED HEN

by Patricia and Fredrick McKissack

The Little Red Hen asks the cat, the dog, and the pig for help. Will it be too late when they stop saying "No"? Find out why saying "I will" can be fun!

Coretta Scott King Award

BUT NOT LIKE MINE

by Margery Facklam

What makes you special? Read about some things you and animals have that are the same. Look for a surprise at the end!

Outstanding Science Trade Book

THEME

Just Like Me

What are the things you like to do best? Read about some boys and girls who are special, just like you.

CONTENTS

9

AWARD-WINNING
AUTHOR/
ILLUSTRATOR

SHARED READING

Quick as a Cricket

by Audrey Wood

illustrated by Don Wood

I'm as quick as a cricket,

I'm as slow as a snail,

I'm as small as an ant,

I'm as large as a whale.

I'm as sad as a basset,

I'm as happy as a lark,

I'm as nice as a bunny,

I'm as mean as a shark.

I'm as cold as a toad,

I'm as hot as a fox,

I'm as weak as a kitten,

I'm as strong as an ox.

I'm as loud as a lion,

I'm as quiet as a clam,

I'm as tough as a rhino,

I'm as gentle as a lamb.

I'm as brave as a tiger,

I'm as shy as a shrimp,

I'm as tame as a poodle,

I'm as wild as a chimp.

I'm as lazy as a lizard,

I'm as busy as a bee,

Put it all together,

And you've got ME!

Willoughby, Wallaby, Woo

by Dennis Lee • illustrated by Jennie Oppenheimer

Willoughby, Wallaby, Woo,
An elephant sat on you!
Willoughby Wallaby Wee,
An elephant sat on me.

Willoughby, Wallaby, Wob,
An elephant sat on Bob.
Willoughby Wallaby Wommy,
An elephant sat on Tommy.

AWARD-WINNING
AUTHOR/
ILLUSTRATOR

SHARED READING

MY
FRIENDS
by Taro Gomi

I learned to walk from my friend
the cat.

I learned to jump from my friend the dog.

I learned to climb from my friend
the monkey.

I learned to run from my friend
the horse.

49

I learned to march from my friend the rooster.

I learned to nap from

my friend the crocodile.

I learned to smell the flowers
from my friend the butterfly.

I learned to hide from

my friend the rabbit.

I learned to explore the earth from

my friend the ant.

I learned to kick from my friend
the gorilla.

I learned to watch the night sky
from my friend the owl.

I learned to sing from my friends
the birds.

I learned to read from

my friends the books.

I learned to study from

my friends the teachers.

I learned to play from

my friends at school.

And I learned to love from
a friend like you.

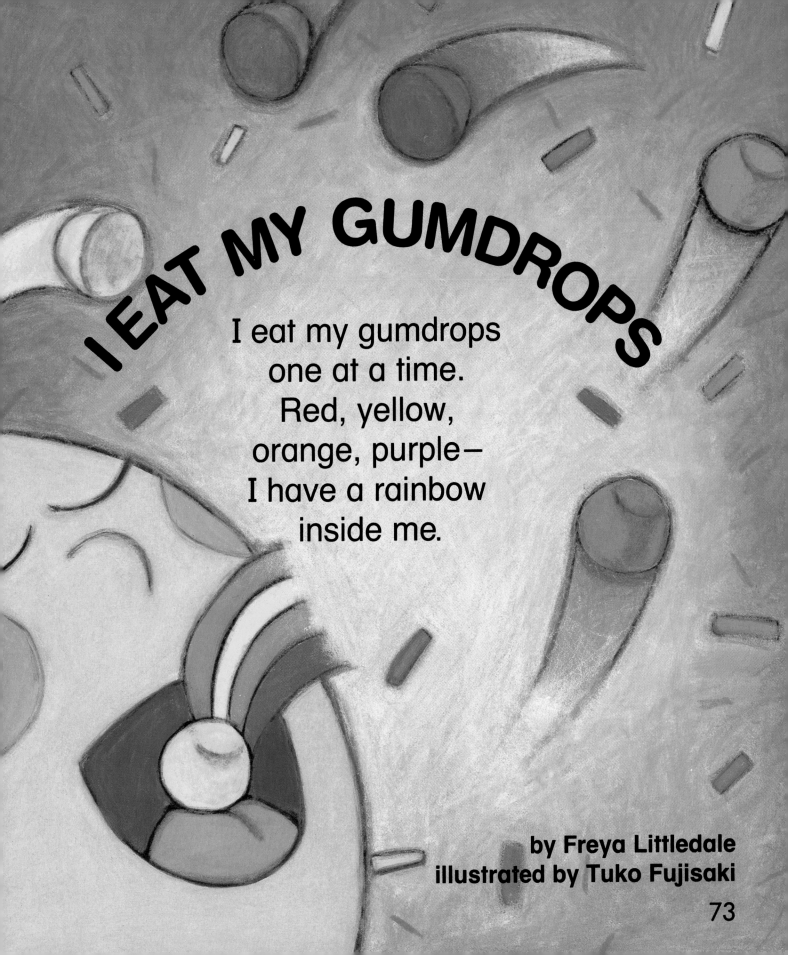

I EAT MY GUMDROPS

I eat my gumdrops
one at a time.
Red, yellow,
orange, purple—
I have a rainbow
inside me.

by Freya Littledale
illustrated by Tuko Fujisaki

73

AWARD-WINNING
POET

I Can

by Mari Evans

I can
be anything
I can
do anything
I can
think
anything
big
or tall
or

high or low

WIDE

or narrow

fast or s l o w

because

I CAN

and

**I
WANT
TO!**

Counting

Lee Bennett Hopkins

AWARD-WINNING AUTHOR

1-2
I love you.

3-4
I love you more.

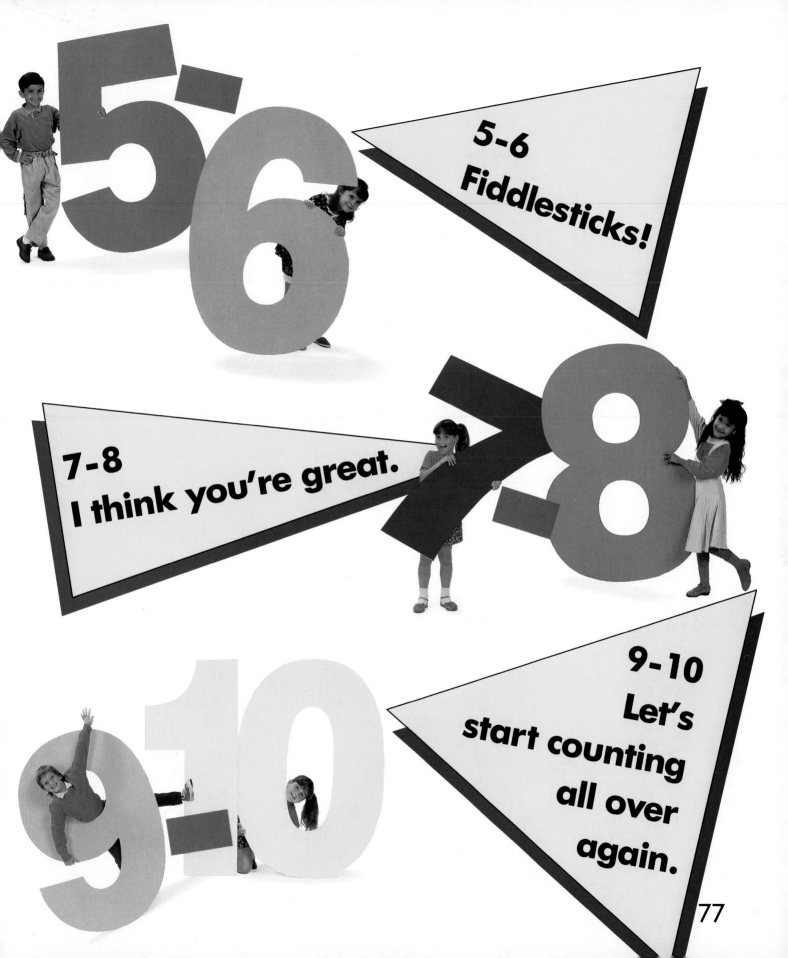

5-6
Fiddlesticks!

7-8
I think you're great.

9-10
Let's start counting all over again.

77

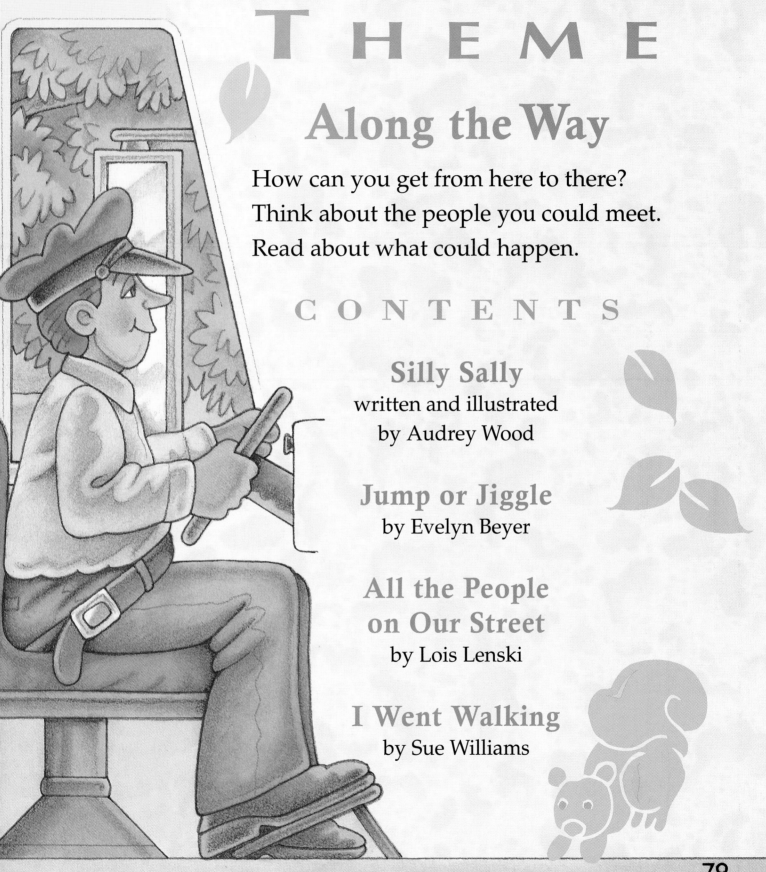

T H E M E

Along the Way

How can you get from here to there?
Think about the people you could meet.
Read about what could happen.

C O N T E N T S

Silly Sally went to town,
walking backwards, upside down.

On the way she met a pig,
a silly pig,

they danced a jig.

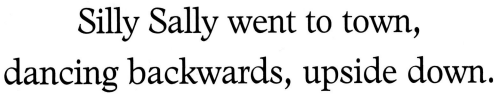

Silly Sally went to town,
dancing backwards, upside down.

87

On the way she met a dog,
a silly dog,

they played leap-frog.

Silly Sally went to town,
leaping backwards, upside down.

On the way she met a loon,
a silly loon,

they sang a tune.

Silly Sally went to town,
singing backwards, upside down.

Now how did Sally get to town,
sleeping backwards, upside down?

Along came Neddy Buttercup,
walking forwards, right side up.

He tickled the pig
who danced a jig.

He tickled the dog
who played leap-frog.

He tickled Sally
who woke right up.

She tickled Neddy Buttercup.

And that's how Sally got to town,

walking backwards, upside down.

JUMP OR JIGGLE

written by
Evelyn Beyer
illustrated by
Sal Murdocca

Frogs jump
Caterpillars hump
Worms wiggle
Bugs jiggle
Rabbits hop
Horses clop
Snakes slide
Sea gulls glide
Mice creep
Deer leap
Puppies bounce
Kittens pounce
Lions stalk —
But —
I walk!

AWARD-WINNING AUTHOR

All the People on Our Street

All the people on our street

Are people that I like to meet.

I like to walk and say hello

To all the people that I know.

by Lois Lenski

illustrated by Keaf Holliday

3

I went walking.

What did you see?

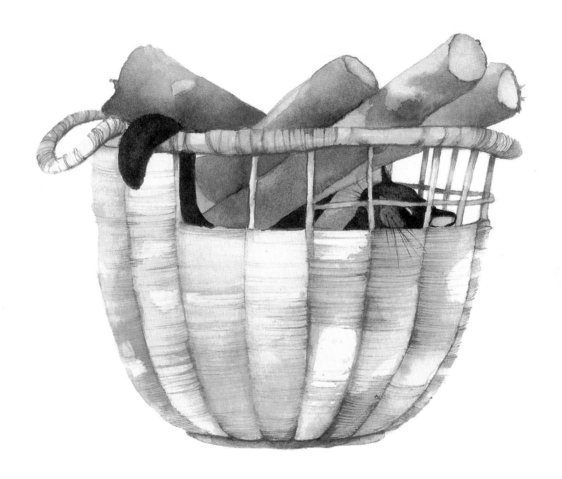

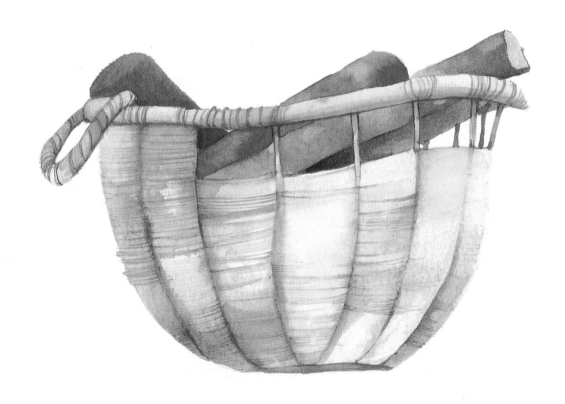

I saw a black cat
Looking at me.

I went walking.

What did you see?

I saw a brown horse
Looking at me.

I went walking.

What did you see?

I saw a red cow
Looking at me.

I went walking.

What did you see?

I saw a green duck
Looking at me.

I went walking.

What did you see?

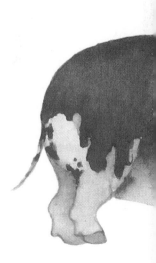

I saw a pink pig
Looking at me.

I saw a yellow dog
Looking at me.

I went walking.

What did you see?

I saw a lot of animals
Following me!